My Island
The Land of Sunshine

by Beverly E. Dyer-Groves

illustrated by Beverly E. Dyer-Groves and Thalia A. Lennon

To order additional copies of this book, contact:
Xlibris
1-888-795-4274
www.Xlibris.com
Orders@Xlibris.com

ISBN: 978-1-4363-9002-6 (sc)
ISBN: 978-1-7960-7729-2 (e)

Print information available on the last page

Rev. date: 12/09/2019

To the following people with many thanks
for your help and inspirations:

- Margo La Gattuta – Instructor
- Shanna M. Groves – My daughter
- Amanda Branch – My friend
- Yanique S. Lee – My niece

Foreword

As an elementary student, I was deeply inspired by my late principal, Edna L. Morris of Mocho Primary School, Clarendon Jamaica. She taught the general subject areas at that time in the upper grades. She was an excellent teacher in singing folk music, playing the piano and writing poetry. She was also a great pianist for the school as well as for the church. I remember her clearly as if it were yesterday.

The class performances over the years allowed us to enter the annual competition which took place in the capital, Kingston. At the end of each performance, the class won many gold, silver and bronze medals. The school was highly recognized throughout the island.

My interest in poetry was renewed four years ago in a creative writing class at Baker College, Auburn Hills. In July, 2007, I entered a contest with one of my poems to The International Library of Poetry, and I was awarded the prestigious Editor's Choice Award for the poem, 'Cherries.' The award further motivated me to write my own book of poems. In the past, I wrote for the opinion section of the local newspaper, The Oakland Press, where I was published a few times.

I like to write for fun and to share my experience, knowledge with anyone who may have an interest in reading. My goal and love of writing continues.

Beverly E. Dyer-Groves

Contents

CHAPTER ONE

Memory

"What we remember from childhood we remember forever-
permanent ghosts, stamped, inked, imprinted, eternally seen."

~ Cynthia Ozick.

JAMAICA, THE LAND I LOVE

I remember things like the gorgeous mountains,
The green valleys that spread out like
Colorful velvet sheets, the land formations
And the various palm trees and other trees
Of beauty that await my arrival any time of the year.
Other moments awaiting me are the white
Sandy beaches along the north coast of the island.
This beauty awaits me calmly and patiently
Especially between September and June

The hills, plateau, and valleys produce
Some of the best coffee, sweetest fruits
And food crops I can ever imagine. These
Products are accompanied by the most
Wonderful sunshine and sunset I will enjoy.
It is beautiful and stunning. It captivates
Every bit of your moments, and when you
Get there and return home, you will say,
"Oh, my goodness, I cannot wait to get back!"

RIPE MANGOES

Happiness is a ripe mango.
I allow the sunshine to
Take care of it while I
Relax and close my eyes
And enjoy every bit of it.
Oh! That yellow and sweet
Tasty feeling tickles my throat
And makes me yearn for more.
It's hard to resist such happiness—
The colorful fruits of red,
Yellow, green or gold.
They sometimes stand in great big bowls
Along the winding roadsides, or
Sometimes on big or small
Mango trees waiting for someone
To own such happiness as her own.
I giggle and I laugh
As every summer draws near
Because I am sure my mind
Will be at ease in this season,
Gulping down the thick juicy
Happiness as I lie on the soft
Seat under the cool, shaded tree.

SUGAR CANE

As sweet as syrup
As sweet as honey
Slumping like a bear,
In the shape of its container.
Blue ribbon
Yellow ribbon
Just to name a few,
Healthy long joints.
Soft as sponge between the teeth
Fresh from the field
Big and juicy
In roots of ten or more.
Fat and robust,
They lean on each other,
When the cool wind blows
As they support each other.
At the time of harvest
Their masters made
Them into blocks of sugar,
Bottles of juices, syrup and rum.
How can I forget the days
When my siblings, friends and I
Sat and ate the sweet juicy cane?
Those days sure left memories lingering.

CHERRIES

The smell of red cherries
Smells like fresh flowers.
Lovely lasting fragrance
Makes one feel joyful.
The aroma penetrates the nostril,
Thinking of springtime in the fall
The perfect time to view the field,
And watch the tasty fruit mature
With exciting, cheerful colors
That make one gaze and gaze.
Birds in high treetops twitter
Melodious songs that are pleasing
To the ear as the wind blows softly.
Oh, springtime! Come again, come again;
Let us look merry like cherries on the tree.

CHERISH THE MOMENTS

Cherish the moments
Moments that bring laughter
Moments that bring fears
Moments that you favor,
Especially in your childhood days.
How can you forget them?
They are there to stay as long
As your memory lasts.
Great moments of reflection
Linger on as life goes on.

GROWING UP

As a child, I was raised humbly,
Respectfully with family and community.
I didn't have a lot of joy,
Gadgets, or manufactured toys!
Instead, I created telephone toys
And pony riding from empty cans,
Strings, green sticks or dry sticks,
Which I cracked on the rock.
Elementary schooling was unforgettable
I got some terrible whippings
With tears dripping for time tables.
Parts of speech stood tall and memorable.
I never thought of complaining to Mom
When I came from school because
I would get punishment to be cool
And to support the teacher's rule.
As I grew up, and experienced maturity,
I migrated to various places,
And I met people of different races.
Culturally, people make a difference.
Some people lack respect.
As a matured adult, I won't forget.
I still like some ways I was raised
Without a doubt or regret.
Moral values are highly shared,
From the youngest to the oldest.
Looking back in my childhood days,
Life is full of changes in many ways.

WHAT IS JOY?

Joy is stewed chicken.
It's delicious with different seasonings.
You can marinate it overnight.
It is satisfying to everyone.
Joy is jerked chicken.
How do you prepare it?
It's appetizing and lip smacking.
Give me some more, please.
Joy is fried chicken,
And you know it's good.
It's easy to prepare for a party dish.
Oh! The smell is driving me crazy!
Joy is baked chicken.
Whenever it's ready,
The aroma will keep you
On your toes to check it out.
Joy is curried chicken,
Chopped in small pieces
And seasoned with curry and others.
Well, whatever ways it's done,
Joy will always be there.

PICTURES

Pictures are wonderful to keep.
They can also take you to places
that you have never gone in your lifetime.
They improve your imagination
And help you to focus on a brighter tomorrow.

Pictures help you in the justice
System by viewing, interpreting and
concluding the results. No wonder
A picture is worth a thousand words
in cases, whether simple or difficult.

FRIENDS

Joyful,   loving,   friendly,

Close   like   two   peas   in   a   pod.

Closeness   turns   to   resentment.

Staring,   angry

Enemies.

CHAPTER TWO

LOVE

"To love is to receive a glimpse of heaven."

~Karen Sunde.

WELCOME

Former students all welcome you
With great enthusiasm.
The feeling is just fantastic,
The warm hugs and the hearty laughter.
It's just amazing and exciting.
The experience of meeting with friends, co-workers
And others is just astonishing.
It is a super, warm-hearted feeling.
This welcome is like visiting close, loving family
Whom you haven't seen for many years.
Even past students stop, greet and remind you of
Some treats you gave them, treats that you have forgotten
Sharing with them some time or other.
No wonder it is said that people remember how
You treat them long after you meet them.

WHEN WE SMILE

When we smile, our facial muscles relax.
Smiling is a sign of happiness and contentment.
When we smile, the world smiles back at us.
There are thousands of people who would like
To smile as much as we do, but many of them
Just can't make it.
Smiling is taught even at our first year in school,
But not everyone learns everything at the
Same time or the same rate.
And we know that, in life, we are never too
Old to learn something we want to learn.
So let's learn to be happy. Learn to smile
When it is appropriate.
Our facial muscle relax, and even if we
Speak a different language, it is all right to smile
Because when we wear a pleasant smile,
We can open up a world.

KEYS

Keys open locks on doors.
Keys open knowledge
To better understanding.
Keys keep secret safe and sound.
Keys secure our lives from danger.
Are there keys to the lonely heart?

GENTLE CARING

With a cheerful smile
You will be bound to receive
When you enter the window
To sign in and receive treatment.

With the most caring voice,
You are absolutely welcome
And asked to rate the pain
From zero through ten.
Bear in mind that zero
Is the best number
And ten is the worst.

The tone of voice,
The gentle hands,
The kindest words
Along with the activities
And medications used
Start the healing process.

The stretching and bending,
The abduction and adduction,
The rotation of upper and lower joints,
The ultra sound and heating pack
Continue the healing process.

A process of being professionally
Cared for brings along
Results which are satisfying
To the patient who seeks
recuperation.

Team work and dedication are clearly
noticeable.
Leaving the facility, each visit
calculates
The body's achievement.
A patient's readiness and involvement
Surely and truly are great necessities.
Thank goodness for caring human
beings.

29

THE PRESENCE OF LOVE

Love has a lasting feeling and a caring heart.
When love is present, someone has compassion
And that person is ready to forgive a friend.
The presence of love displays a calming voice,
Sincerity, kindness and understanding.
Love carries no envy or grudge, instead
It carries peace, tranquility and harmony.
Love is always willing to share thoughts
And itself to observers and desirable ones.

PEACE

Is quietness
Free from disturbance and war,

Peace of mind
Tranquility that others long for.

To be at peace with yourself, friends,
Neighbors is a wonderful achievement.
Peace allows you to expand and improve your
Imagination as much as you want
When peace is at hand.

Your peace of mind allows calmness and relaxation.
Peace of mind makes you
Reminisce on the past,
Focus on the present and
Plan for the future to make it a success.

Peace in your life with the set goals in mind
Will produce the end result of
The best achievements you can ever imagine.
Yes! Peace is here to stay as long as
You can grasp it.

ENJOYMENT

It makes little or no sense
Working endlessly and storing
Riches for enjoyment when you
Get older or when you retire.

What seems to make sense is
While you continue to work hard,
Take vacations in between.
It is a wonderful feeling.

Go sightseeing, view the world
And experience the beauty of
The ocean, mountains, landscape,
Animals and plants of all descriptions,
Flowers and fruits. Architectural works
And designs await your company to take
Your deep moments and your breath away.

These moments and wanders yearn
For you with warm hearts and cuddling arms.
Wait no longer; life does not stay with us forever,
So make your plans now.
Do not store your labor to enjoy it later
Because tomorrow may never come and
Time waits for no man.

SISTER

You are the love of my life,
My best friend.

Sometimes misunderstood,
At times I was jealous of your
Fair skin and your success,
Dying to be like you,
But you are my sister.

For the differences we have
I cannot change.
I will cherish the time
We shared a room.

I looked at you with envy,
As everything you touched prospered.
The compliments you got from
Mum and Dad were like swords to my heart.

I was bruised for the injustice you never brought on me.
My insecurities with guys came from
When only you were noticed and adored,
For how cute you looked.

But now that I am old and grey,
You're still loved so dearly,
For during all those times
You remained my sister and loved me.

GENUINE FRIENDS

They are God's sent angels
The ones who will be there
In good times and other times,

The ones who are there
When you most need them
For support, love and advice,
Consultation and ideas.

Genuine friends are there
For you always, and even
When they pass on, their works
And images are unforgettable.

FAMILY

Family members are the closest ones to you
In jovial times and heart-rending times.
A family member is your greatest support
When you most need someone to
Listen to you, grieve with you and comfort you.

When you are glum, family will uplift you
With great words of encouragement,
And when you achieve your goal, family
Will celebrate your success with difficult work.

Some family members keep your secrets,
Guide and protect you from inconsiderate ones.
A loving and caring family doesn't care whether
You are penniless or penny wealthy, but this family
Will always accept you for who you are.
Thoughtful family members will be there when
You are most in need of them.

CHAPTER THREE

Nature

"Let us permit nature to have her way.
She understands her business better than we do."

~Michel de Montaigne.

NATURE

It is no guarantee
What nature can do.
Nature is beautiful
But sometimes it
Can turn deadly.

When a hurricane or a
Tornado slams unexpectedly
Across the unprepared country,
Its short notice does not
Lend enough time to seek refuge
Or get out of harm's way.

It is scary and dangerous,
Heart breaking and nerve racking
For pleasure seekers, hikers and
Astronauts, just to name a few.
Gloomy moments, irresistible weather

Bravery and self-determination
Are parts of the internal's instinct
Of fierce and willing soul.
Nature brings loss of lives,
Shelter, clothing, and foods
To men's fruitful harvests.
Starvation and suffering creep in
When nature rages highly.

Nature brings about regret,
Mourning, sorrow and disbelief
As well as joy, excitement,
And wonder to us all.
Nature rules the world
Whenever she wants to
As long as she wants to.

THE SEASONS

Why do you have four seasons and others may have one?
If you can answer the question, then do not worry about it,
But it's a wonderful experience to watch them all when
You know they are on their way, one behind the other.

I still enjoy watching snowflakes falling like raindrops
On leafless branches in winter.
It is exciting to have all four,
'cause other places may have one season or maybe two or three.

A season can creep in gently like a baby, and other times it can rush in
Like a roaring lion. Seasons can inter-twine whenever they want to.
Springtime comes in winter, and winter comes in spring.
Summer comes in fall and fall comes in summer.

You adapt to any season whenever and in what ever form
It presents itself.
Everyone critiques seasons daily, but they are still loved
By the majority in every shape or form.

WHAT ABOUT TREES?

Trees are beautiful and beneficial to us.
They come in various sizes, shapes and colors.
We depend on trees and trees depend on us.
Trees inhale carbon dioxide and exhale oxygen,
And animals inhale oxygen and exhale carbon dioxide.

Fewer trees in a neighborhood produce
An unhealthy or unsafe environment.
When trees are destroyed, little and big
Creatures are driven away, roaming and wandering
In search of new habitats as their resting ground.

Trees are lifesavers for living creatures
Whether they are big or small.
Trees have served numerous purposes since
The beginning of creation.

THE BODY

It's a God-given gift to you.
Do not abuse it.
Take care and consideration.
You have only one body,
A body that protects all
The important organs inside
that are not easily replaced.

As you live on, pay attention
To what is ingested; if not, the
result can be regretful and devastating.

Before you partake of anything,
Remember, you have one body,
A body that is unique and a body
that is irreplaceable.

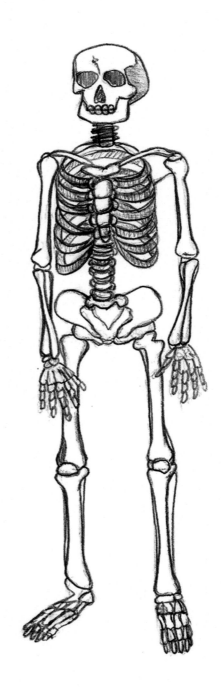

A FARM POND

I lie calm and quiet
Sometimes as clear as crystal
And seldom annoyed by unfriendly guests
Who always come to taste of me.

When showers of rain pour down
I am relaxed and fill with contentment,
But I am thankful that I am a lifesaver.
I am like a supernatural being

Found in every particle of foods.
Cows, pigs, hens, and ducks
Use me incessantly, as I'm
Always available to be used.

There's another special fact about me.
I can change into different forms.
At times I'm like a rock
But I can be a vapor as well,

But regardless of my form,
I enjoy viewing the world.
I am available for my master
Who always depends on me.

COLD AIR

Cold air is there.
It brings much fear
How dare you dress
In such light clothing
Knowing the future
Outcome of what can
Take place in your body?

Let's prepare to face
The cold air, as autumn
Creeps in with its beautiful,
Vibrant and variegated colors,
While the cold air gets colder and colder.

HARVEST TIME

It's a festive season
That is generally
Enjoyed by happy people
Throughout the entire globe,
Whether we are from the
East, west, north or south.

A time to reap, a time
To eat, a time to celebrate
And a time to preserve
The end product we have gathered.

Our loved ones are cheerful
And they look forward to celebrate
With a glorious season of
Peace, love and tranquility.

APPLES

Apples are colorful and beautiful
And have colors that are red, green or gold.
Some apples are as sweet as sugar,
And some are as sour as lime,
But regardless of the taste
You won't let them waste.

Apples are used in baking.
The sauce is tasty for even a baby.
When eaten as a snack,
The pie is delicious.
When served as a desert,
Surely you won't be hurt.

Apples make a great drink
And allow the mind to think
About such wonderful fruit.
This fruit exists way back
In the story of the creation,
A story that is as old as a hill.

There is an old saying,
"An apple a day
Keeps the doctor away."
Maybe it is one fruit,
Which has fewer calories
When you munch it,
When your teeth crunch it.
It is good for a meal
No matter how you partake of it.

NONSENSE POEM

THE ZOO

Elephants,igerts, blama, and giglets
Early womblingri
Up and back and forth
Mussops go inside.

Swagle, gabble, umble
Lazy dazy, toasted days
Reevls,lemac,arbez too
Gabbles, swaggle, umble through.

Slaebs, raebs, tacs and tars
Mingle unaware
Lowger, womie, snickle back
Knowing not to care.

Grungry, lungry, nettle in
Snoogled, woogled warm and glin.
Night falls, owls call.
All are safe within.

DOGS ARE SPECIAL

Dogs are man's best friend
And they will be to the end.
They've played such important parts
In man's life from the beginning of
Time until even now and through
   their lifetime.

They pull sleds and work like slaves
In snowy, cold and dreary weather.
Some dogs are trained to lead the blind.
They bring in their master's mail
And soon after wag their tail.

Dogs are even trained to do
Exceptional jobs in the justice system.
They sometimes become whistle
   blowers
And help bring justice to the unjust ones.
Oh, what wonderful creatures they are!

Dogs give their masters hints
And make them aware of enemies
Who are close by to attack direct
Ones or loved ones in a neighborhood.
No wonder they are man's best friend.

For a job that is well done,
Its master gives the dog a treat
As it relaxes quietly by his feet,
And chews on its yummy biscuit
During its favorite snack time of the day.

When dogs are unhappy, we will know
   by their actions
And by their unpleasant motions.
They will act like sad children and yearn
For attention, but regardless of their
   actions
They are known as man's best friend.

KITCHEN KNIVES

The kitchen soldiers stand
Tall in the brown wooden block,
Where her master had them locked.
Great lasting kitchen knives
Like to be used by the industrious wives.
They keep them really shiny
Like the twinkling stars above.
A kitchen without a sharp knife
Is like a gentle soul without a wife

WEARING HATS

Hats are worn and used for different reasons.
People wear hats for medical benefits, choices,
To get rid of colds and aches, as a part of their
Uniform, for decoration and beautification,
For color coordination and special occasion.
Others wear them to hide funny hair styles, crooked ears
Or foreheads, or unkempt, discolored hair.

But whatever reason, a hat is worn for the season.
You must be proud of it as long as it satisfies
The inner soul and it is pleasing to you.

One day I saw my cousin got dressed for a clubhouse
Party. I wasn't sure it was him, so I pulled him aside nicely
And asked him in a whispering voice,
"Can you take your hat off for a second, 'cause I can't
Believe you're looking so hot in your pretty, spanking hat."

THE DRUM

Sounding the drum
Brings a lot of fun,
As I stamp my feet
To the rhythm of the beat.

I bow my head,
I snap my fingers.
The rhythm of the beat
Surely it's a defeat.

Now the rhythm of the beat,
Controls the whole body.
The rhythm of the beat
Is a one time treat.

I am sad to know
When the music stops.
Because the rhythm of the beat
Is in my head nonstop.

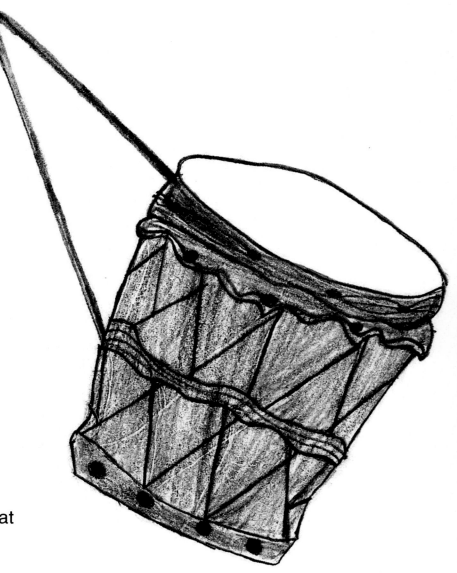

SNOW (Haiku)

Snow cold and fluffy
Lying softly sound asleep
Play with me today.

BIRDS (Haiku)

Dazzling high above
Soaring like non-stop jet plane
Unforgettable!

CHAPTER FOUR

FEAR

"The oldest and strongest emotion of mankind is fear."

H. P. Lovecraft

FEAR

Fear is like wild horses galloping along
My shaky system.
The horses come in quiet darkness.

Go away, you are making me nervous!
I feel like riding you, but my inner spirit is full of fear.
My thoughts are drifting, but I won't let your
Flying hooves control me.

I know my horses are present, and I dare not let them
Have it all,

Because I need a wild horse in my life at some time
Or other to protect and guide me from some danger or
From someone.

FIRE

Fire is hot.
It can burn.
If you are like a fire,
Then you must be hot
May be hot tempered
Or really short tempered.

Fire burns, fire hurts,
But yet it keeps us warm
When we are cold.
It cooks the food
For us to partake
Two or three meals a day.

Fire gives us signals
For rescuers to find us.
There are terrified moments
When awful tears are shed.

Fire plays a role in celebration
Where people gather together
Singing, joking and laughing
Around the warm campfire,

As everyone sits and digests
The sweet and brown
marshmallows
Prepared by helpful hands and
The heat of the fire.

PAIN

You cannot see the pain
But you can feel the pain,
And no one else can feel it except you
Who are experiencing the pain.

At each and every hour,
You need the Supreme Power
To bless, improve, and uphold
Your faith to bear the pain.

As you wait hopefully and humbly
For a better feeling because the Supreme
Being has power and control over
The given body you are blessed with,

You look forward to a better hour,
A better tomorrow and more
Prosperous days to come.
You continue to wait patiently.

Thank God for knowledge,
Gifted hands and caring hearts
And other caring workers who
Bring along relief from pain
For you to enjoy fun and fitness again.

WAR

Ugly,   brutal

Sad   as   the   gray   sky

Bullets   and   missiles   turn   ugly

Weeping,   Mourning

Peace

SILENCE

Silence can be used as
A command that goes with
Self-control and body language.
In whatever ways you use it,
Silence can express something
About you or your situation.

Silence can work as
The answer to some questions
And some statements or concerns.
At other times, it pays to be verbal
Or defensive to maintain your rights.
For a peaceful environment,
Silence can become the perfect answer,
And ignorance and war disappear like lightning.

BEING BRAVE

Never be fearful
Never be shy.
If you know that you are truthful,
Then you must show you are brave.
Believe in yourself and be strong
Because in the end you will
Be proud of who you are
Others will be proud of you as well.

IT WASN'T BEAUTIFUL

It wasn't beautiful, but he loved life,
A life that may be boring,
A life that may be filled with
Hope and dreams for
A super bright fantastic future.
He thought quite often
About his optimistic life.
To be a millionaire, he would be
Happy as a king on a throne.
He never got real discouraged
Because his life was full of
courage.

BEYOND BORDERS

Think to learn more of the world
Around you every day.
Go outside of your frontier
And learn the different ways of life.
Learn about other people of different cultures.
Learning more about people in the world
Is astounding, informative and remarkable.

There are people who are not even exposed
To much civilization, and many who
Strive to find their next meal for the day.
They remain hopeful and thankful to be alive,
So when you think that life is difficult,
Learn more facts about other cultures.
This will teach you to be more thankful for
Family, friends and others in your life.

CHAPTER FIVE

Success

"When you have to make a choice
and don't make it, that is in itself a choice."

~ William James

FOLLOW YOUR DREAM

To follow your dream
Is your greatest gift,
But you must be strong
Never think you are wrong.

Your self determination
Without any frustration
Can be easily achieved
Just by patient trying.

So, follow your dream,
Allow no one to scream.
Of the achiever's team
By following your dream.

ATTITUDE

You spring into my mind without a hint
Like a big great monster.
Attitude, you didn't think of the question
Before you replied in a disgusted manner.
You have no thought or sympathy.
Why did you do that?
You are a fearless creature
And that is so ridiculous.
Attitude, you must vanish now.
I am ashamed of your behavior
And the way you portray yourself.
I am not excited about you in my life.
If you want to be with me, you will
Have to turn to a new page.
My mind is already made up.
Show me the best of what you are
And you will be mine forever and
Forever or until the end of time.

T-SHIRT

My T-Shirt is yellow
Given to me by a fellow.
It is bright as
The sun that shines
Like a brand new coin.
The T-Shirt makes me
Feel special and mellow.

I like bright, brilliant color.
It always cheers me up
If there is unpleasant feeling
In what appears as dishonest dealing.

T-Shirts are worn several times
To celebrate team spirit joyfully
And the pride of working
Together with significant others.

GIFTS

Each one of you is born with a gift or two . . .
It's up to you to make the best use of them.
Many times you have lots of hidden talents hanging around
Just waiting for a spark to step up to the plate,
For you to welcome them and have them put to some amazing,
Exciting and jaw-dropping wonders to admire.
Entertainers and pleasure-seekers have never thought of such moments.
When you think that you are great at something you are doing,
Embrace the gifts; success is just around the corner
Waiting for you gracefully, waiting for you to hold and treasure them.

WHO SAID IT COULDN'T BE DONE?

How many times do you
Have to prove it, that it can
Be done just by patient trying?
You have to first of all
Believe in yourself—that you
Can change the impossible.

And all that is happening
Comes from the inner spirit
That dwells inside the body,
The body that solely belongs to you.
When someone says, "It can't be done!"
Prove to the world, it's a folly.

Be strong with a determined mind;
Believe in yourself magnificently.
You cannot afford to throw in the towel.
When help is needed, seek it.
It is splendid and marvelous
To say, "Yes, I have accomplished it
With joy and pleasure."

DON'T SETTLE FOR LESS

Aim for the star always.
You should never give up.
You have too much potential.
Too much time will be at waste.
When time and work seem difficult
It's a hint that you are getting what
You are striving hard to achieve.

There are more pessimists in your
Life than there are optimists,
But tell yourself, "I can do it and
I will make it."

Focus on your dreams with a positive
Attitude because you have new potentials
That are still unknown.

You will surprise yourself about
Your new discoveries.
So, always work with a positive mind
And don't you dare settle for less.

Printed in the United States
By Bookmasters